Original title:
Dancing Echoes

Copyright © 2024 Creative Arts Management OÜ
All rights reserved.

Author: Amelia Montgomery
ISBN HARDBACK: 978-9916-90-596-8
ISBN PAPERBACK: 978-9916-90-597-5

Harmonies of the Heartbeat

In the quiet of the night,
Soft whispers take their flight.
Beats align like stars above,
A melody of gentle love.

Eyes meet in tender grace,
Time stands still in this space.
Each pulse a note, pure and true,
Harmonies of me and you.

Flickering Footfalls

Through the forest, shadows play,
Footfalls dance along the way.
Whispers of the leaves in sway,
Nature's song, a sweet ballet.

Echoes of a fleeting light,
Guiding us through the night.
Every step, a story spun,
Flickering like the setting sun.

Woven Echoes of Time

Threads of past and future blend,
In every moment, we suspend.
Memories like leaves do fall,
Woven echoes, we recall.

Time's fabric, richly spun,
Patterns bright, begun and done.
Each heartbeat a stitch in fate,
Woven tales that we create.

The Dance of Fleeting Moments

In the twilight, shadows glide,
Moments swirl, a gentle tide.
Time's embrace, we twirl and sway,
Dancing through the light of day.

Each heartbeat counts, a breath, a sigh,
Fleeting whispers, passing by.
In this dance, we find our way,
Moments cherished, never stray.

The Pulse of Twilight

The sun dips low, a fading glow,
Colors blend, where dreams do flow.
An evening sigh, the world holds still,
Whispers soft, a night so chill.

Stars awaken, twinkle bright,
In this calm, the heart takes flight.
Shadows dance in gentle breeze,
Time slows down, the mind finds ease.

Steps Beneath the Stars

Footfalls echo on the ground,
With each step, new worlds are found.
The cosmos watches from up high,
As wishes linger, dreams will fly.

Paths entwined in silver light,
Guided softly into night.
The universe, a silent guide,
In its embrace, we do confide.

Choreography of Dreams

In slumber's grasp, the mind takes flight,
Dancing through the velvet night.
A waltz of hopes, a ballet sweet,
Where heart and spirit softly meet.

Each step a tale, a whispered song,
In this realm, we all belong.
The moonlight shines, a stage so grand,
In dreams, we leap, we understand.

Silhouettes in the Night

Figures linger, dark and slight,
Sketches drawn in shades of night.
With fleeting grace, they come alive,
In soft twilight, they twist and strive.

Echoes murmur through the air,
Secrets held in whispered prayer.
Shape and shadow, hand in hand,
In dreams, they dance across the land.

Swaying to Infinity

In a field of whispers, I dance alone,
Beneath the vast sky, a heart full of tone.
Each blade of grass sways in gentle embrace,
Time drifts away in this sacred space.

Stars twinkle above, like dreams in the night,
Pulling me closer to the realm of light.
With every soft breath, I feel my soul soar,
Swaying to rhythms I can't help but explore.

Feathers on the Wind

Feathers drift softly, caressed by the breeze,
Carrying whispers among the tall trees.
Each flutter a story of journeys begun,
A dance with the skies, a race with the sun.

In the quiet moments, they find their true path,
Wandering freely, escaping the wrath.
Softly they tumble, like thoughts set afloat,
Feathers on the wind, in dreams they wrote.

The Language of Light

Light spills like laughter on the canvas of space,
Painting with colors, each hue finds its place.
Flickers of warmth in the chill of the night,
Whispers of hope in the heartbeats of light.

A symphony crafted in radiant beams,
Translating the silence into luminous dreams.
In every reflection, a story so bright,
Telling the tales in the language of light.

Sonic Footprints

Echoes resound with each step that I take,
Tracing the moments, each stamp, every break.
Notes dance in chaos, a melody spun,
Sonic footprints left as the day is begun.

In the silence that follows, I hear the refrain,
Of laughter and sorrow, of joy and of pain.
Each sound a reminder of where I have been,
Sonic footprints marking the places within.

The Cadence of Connection

In whispers soft, we intertwine,
A dance of souls, in rhythm divine.
With every breath, our spirits sway,
Bound by the threads of yesterday.

Through laughter shared, and sorrow's song,
We find the places where we belong.
In silent glances, our hearts converse,
Each moment cherished, a timeless verse.

Like echoes in the evening air,
Our stories weave, a tapestry rare.
With gentle hands, we craft our fate,
In every heartbeat, connections generate.

In twilight's glow, our shadows blend,
A melody sweet that will never end.
Together we stand, through thick and thin,
In the cadence of love, we always begin.

Echoing Dreams of Yesterday

Beneath the stars, where memories play,
Whispers of dreams from yesterday.
In every sigh, the past survives,
A haunting tune that forever thrives.

Through time's embrace, we drift and glide,
Carried by hopes that never hide.
In twilight's glow, the shadows loom,
A tapestry woven, an echo's bloom.

With every heartbeat, the past draws near,
A symphony rich, both distant and clear.
In every flicker of the night sky,
Dreams intertwine, as stars reply.

As morning breaks, the echoes fade,
But in our hearts, the song is laid.
We carry forth the dreams once sown,
In the garden of time, where love has grown.

Pulse of the Unseen

In silence deep, the pulse resides,
A heartbeat felt where truth abides.
Beneath the skin, vibrations flow,
Whispers of life, in shadows glow.

In every breath, the unseen stirs,
Connected threads, where existence blurs.
With every touch, we sense the thread,
A world alive in what's unsaid.

Through twilight veils, we seek and find,
The hidden pulse that binds mankind.
In every moment, a secret shared,
The pulse of the unseen, ever bared.

Together we dance through time and space,
Embracing the mystery of our grace.
In harmony, we rise and bend,
To the pulse of existence, our thoughts transcend.

Harmonic Shadows

In twilight's embrace, shadows play,
A dance of hues that softly sway.
With every flicker, a story's spun,
Harmonic whispers in the fading sun.

As darkness deepens, the chords unite,
Melodies crafting the edge of night.
In the stillness, echoes linger,
A phantom touch, a ghostly singer.

Through silent streets, our footsteps blend,
Harmonic shadows, our spirits mend.
In every corner, a note we trace,
A symphony woven with gentle grace.

Though shadows may fade with the dawn's light,
The harmony lingers, ever in sight.
In silence, we hold what cannot be shown,
In the depths of our hearts, the shadows have grown.

Fluid Echoes of Emotion

Waves crash softly on the shore,
Carrying whispers from the past.
Each drop holds a story untold,
Time's embrace, fleeting yet vast.

Ripples dance under the moon,
Reflecting dreams and old regrets.
Hearts collide like shadows at noon,
In the tide, no one forgets.

Moments flow like streams of grace,
Winding through the valleys of time.
In the current, we find our place,
Each echo a haunting rhyme.

In fluid motion, feeling bends,
Carved in memory's endless sway.
As water meets the earth, it mends,
These echoes never fade away.

A Waltz Through Whispered Memories

Softly we move in the twilight,
Among the shades of long-lost days.
Each step recounts a gentle fight,
In the dance's warm embrace.

Laughter twirls like autumn leaves,
Spinning tales of love and fear.
The music flows, heartache weaves,
In the rhythm, we draw near.

Fragrant dreams in the night air,
Whispers linger on our skin.
Every note leads us to where
Sweet memories first begin.

We waltz beneath a starlit dome,
In each heartbeat, our essence stays.
Together we find a home,
In this dance of endless days.

Twilight's Serenade

The sky blushes in shades of gold,
As day surrenders to the night.
Stars awaken, stories told,
In the hush, the world feels right.

Gentle breezes weave a song,
Whispers of dreams to come alive.
In this moment, we belong,
As twilight's love begins to thrive.

The shadows dance, the light retreats,
Painting silences with grace.
Every heartbeat, a rhythm beats,
In the twilight's warm embrace.

Embrace the calm, let worries fade,
Underneath the cosmic play.
In twilight's glow, our fears evade,
Together, we greet the day.

The Language of Laughter

Bright chuckles ripple through the air,
Painting smiles across the room.
Joy springs forth, beyond compare,
In laughter's light, we bloom.

Each giggle like a soft refrain,
Threads of happiness interlace.
In every burst, joy breaks the chain,
Unity found in each embrace.

Whispers of mirth break the night,
Echoing in the softest sound.
With every joke, the heart takes flight,
In laughter, our solace is found.

For in this language so divine,
All woes can pause, and hope can rise.
With laughter's love, the stars align,
In joy, we find our brightest skies.

Harmonies of Heartbeats

In the quiet, hearts align,
Softly beating, one divine.
Whispers dance in moonlit glow,
In this moment, love will grow.

Fingers trace a gentle path,
Joined in joy, escaping wrath.
Every pulse, a song we share,
Wrapped in warmth, free as air.

Under stars, our dreams ignite,
Promises woven through the night.
Harmony in every breath,
Love transcending life and death.

As the dawn begins to break,
Waking dreams we dared to make.
In the light, our hearts still hum,
In this rhythm, we are one.

Fluidity of Time

Time flows like a gentle stream,
Moments shift, a fleeting dream.
Seconds dance like fluttering leaves,
In their passage, the heart believes.

Memories drift, both sweet and slight,
Echoes of past within the light.
Rivers weave through valleys deep,
In their currents, secrets keep.

Tomorrow whispers in the breeze,
Yesterday fades, its grasp will ease.
Present blooms with colors bright,
In this canvas, life takes flight.

As time spins its endless thread,
We weave stories of love and dread.
Crafted tales in the fabric of fate,
In its hands, we meditate.

Echoes of Laughter

Laughter lingers in the air,
Bubbling joy beyond compare.
Each giggle, like a melody,
Crafting bonds for all to see.

In the park where shadows play,
Children's smiles light up the day.
Chasing dreams through fields so wide,
In this joy, we all confide.

Echoes drift through time and space,
Woven threads of warm embrace.
Every chuckle, every cheer,
Paints the canvas we hold dear.

As the twilight softly falls,
Laughter lifts, a sweet enthrall.
In these moments, pure and true,
Life's great gift, both me and you.

Starlit Reverie

Underneath the night's deep veil,
Whispers of the cosmos sail.
Stars ignite like dreams on fire,
In this stillness, hearts conspire.

Moonlight bathes the world in grace,
Every shadow finds its place.
Sparkling tales in velvet skies,
In their depths, our spirit flies.

Glimmers of a distant past,
Echoes of a love to last.
In this reverie, we dance,
Lost in time, we take our chance.

With each twinkle, hope takes flight,
Guiding souls through silent night.
In the wonder, we embrace,
Every heartbeat, a warm trace.

Ortus of Echoing Hearts

In the dawn's gentle embrace,
Whispers rise from the ground,
Echoes of dreams unforgotten,
In shadows where love is found.

Sky paints hues of soft gold,
As hearts begin to race,
In the warmth of the morning,
Soft laughter fills the space.

Chasing light through the thickets,
Every heartbeat a song,
With each whispered promise,
The world feels less wrong.

As the sun seeks its throne,
In the canvas of blue,
We gather our echoes,
To begin life anew.

Echoes of the Nocturnal Tide

Moonlight spills on the sea,
Whispers ride on the breeze,
Night's embrace gently cradles,
As the world finds its ease.

Stars shimmer like secrets,
In the vast, darkened sky,
Each wave holds a story,
Of dreams that never die.

The tide rolls in with a sigh,
Carrying hopes on its crest,
In the dance of the shadows,
We find solace and rest.

Each echo a reminder,
Of paths yet to roam,
In the stillness of night,
The heart always finds home.

Unraveled Rhythms

In the pulse of the evening,
Rhythms start to unfold,
Each beat is a journey,
Adventures yet untold.

The dance of the twilight,
Swaying with the breeze,
Notes intertwine like lovers,
In a cacophony of ease.

Every heartbeat a story,
Written in the air,
As we spin through the moments,
In a world free of care.

Unraveled and open,
We chase what feels right,
In the music of the stars,
We find our own light.

Flickers of the Celestial Dance

Stars collide in the twilight,
A waltz across the skies,
Galaxies spin and shimmer,
As time silently flies.

In the quiet of the cosmos,
Whispers of fate align,
Each flicker a reminder,
Of love that's so divine.

Meteor trails like dreams,
Cross the curtain of night,
Carving paths through the heavens,
Chasing the fleeting light.

As we watch this dance unfold,
Together, hand in hand,
In the vastness of the universe,
Our hearts take a stand.

Diaphanous Layers of Light

Shadows flicker in the glow,
Waves of color gently flow.
Whispers of dawn softly rise,
Painting dreams against the skies.

Veils of mist on morning's breath,
Each hue dances, defying death.
Sunbeams weave through ancient trees,
Carrying songs upon the breeze.

Glimmers brush the sleepy ground,
In their aura, peace is found.
Nature hums in vibrant tones,
Life awakens, and love moans.

Underneath this radiant dome,
Hearts converge; they find their home.
In diaphanous layers bright,
We find solace in the light.

Enigmatic Steps in the Night

Footfalls echo, soft and clear,
In the darkness, shadows leer.
Mysteries are woven tight,
Underneath the cloak of night.

Stars peer down with watchful eyes,
As whispers dance beneath the skies.
Paths uncertain, veils of gloom,
Each step leads to unknown room.

Silhouettes in vague allure,
The heart races, pulse unsure.
Time holds breath, a silent vow,
In the night, we learn the how.

Moments stretch, a fleeting glance,
Within the dark, we find our chance.
Enigmatic, wild, and free,
In the night, we dare to be.

Undercurrents of Time's Dance

Ripples whisper through the air,
Moments melt without a care.
Seasons twirl in soft embrace,
Life flows forward, leaves no trace.

Tides of memory ebb and swell,
Stories hidden, hard to tell.
In the pulse of each heartbeat,
Time holds secrets, bittersweet.

Dancers swirl in endless round,
Their laughter echoes, sweet, profound.
Chasing shadows, lost and found,
In time's arms, we are all bound.

Yet in this waltz, we must trust,
For every footfall turns to dust.
Undercurrents, smooth and grand,
Guide us gently, hand in hand.

The Symphony of Fleeting Days

Melodies of morning light,
Sparkling softly, pure delight.
Hours glide like birds on wing,
In their dance, the echoes sing.

Afternoon drapes in gold sheen,
Moments breathe, serene and keen.
Time's embrace wraps us in sound,
In this symphony, we are found.

Evening calls with tender grace,
Starlit whispers start to chase.
Notes of twilight fill the air,
In the dusk, we lose our care.

Fleeting days, a tune so rare,
Each breath a song, a whispered prayer.
In the quiet, love's refrain,
Plays forever in joy and pain.

Crescendo in the Shadows

In quiet corners, whispers start,
Where secrets linger, dreams depart.
The shadows dance, a silent show,
In darkened realms, the feelings grow.

A flicker here, a glint of light,
Amidst the gloom, a spark ignites.
With every heartbeat, hopes arise,
A rising tide beneath the skies.

The pulse of night begins to swell,
An echo of the tales they tell.
In dusky hues, the stories bloom,
As shadows merge, dispelling gloom.

Each quiet breath, a sound profound,
In hushed embraces, lost and found.
Oh, hear the call, the silent song,
In shadows deep, where we belong.

Vibration of Souls

In perfect harmony, we sway,
Connected hearts in bright array.
The gentle hum of souls in tune,
Beneath the stars, beneath the moon.

A rhythm flows from deep within,
Where every fracture hints of sin.
We dance to echoes, soft yet strong,
Bound by the magic of our song.

The world around begins to fade,
As whispers weave a warm cascade.
In every breath, vibration sounds,
A symphony where love abounds.

In each embrace, a story spun,
Two souls entwined, forever one.
A heartbeat shared, a pulse divine,
In every note, a love we find.

The Flow of Echoes

In valleys deep, the echoes play,
Their timeless dance in bright ballet.
The mountains sing, the rivers cry,
As nature's voice will never die.

Across the cliffs, a whisper's sigh,
A melody that soars and flies.
Each sound a thread, a binding tie,
In every note, the spirits lie.

The forests hum with songs unseen,
In rustling leaves, the past has been.
With every breeze, a tale will flow,
A legacy of life we know.

Together we, in silence, hear,
The echoes calling, drawing near.
In endless cycles, time will weave,
A tapestry of dreams we believe.

Songs of the Unseen

In twilight hours where shadows pen,
The songs are sung by unknown men.
In whispers soft, in echoes clear,
The music stirs, we pause to hear.

The voices rise, like evening mist,
A haunting beauty, hard to resist.
In every note, a heart concealed,
Where words unspoken are revealed.

Across the night, the rhythms glide,
With fluid grace, they swell and slide.
In secret places, truths unfold,
As timeless tales of love retold.

A symphony, our souls entwined,
In every lyric, fate defined.
Together we, in silence weave,
The songs of life, we dare to believe.

Whispers of Rhythm

In the quiet night they play,
Silent tunes that softly sway.
Echoes carry through the air,
Dancing dreams without a care.

Rustling leaves in gentle breeze,
Whispers float among the trees.
Heartbeat drumming, pulse in time,
Nature's song, a perfect rhyme.

Steps that follow moonlit trails,
In soft shadows, magic veils.
Rhythmic ties that bind us tight,
Lost in whispers, pure delight.

With each note, the world stands still,
Filling hearts with soft goodwill.
In the hush, we find our way,
Whispers of rhythm, night and day.

Shadows on the Floor

Flickering flames cast a glow,
Silhouettes dance, moving slow.
Whispers linger in the light,
Shadows play upon the night.

Footsteps echo, soft and low,
In the stillness, feelings flow.
Memories wrapped in embrace,
Every outline, every trace.

Time stands still in shadow's hold,
Stories whispered, secrets told.
In this dim, where dreams take flight,
Shadows weave the fabric bright.

We find solace, hearts aligned,
In the dance, we're intertwined.
On the floor, beneath the stars,
Shadows hum, reminding ours.

Melodies in Motion

Waves of sound, they rise and fall,
Softly whisper, gently call.
Rhythms pulse through limbs and veins,
Carried forth like summer rains.

Feet that glide on polished ground,
In the air, a harmony found.
Trailing notes that swirl and spin,
In this dance, we breathe within.

Moments blend in perfect time,
Every heartbeat, every rhyme.
Melodies that spark delight,
Lifting spirits through the night.

In the flow of life we sway,
Melodies lead, we'll follow play.
Together bound, we take our flight,
In motion's arms, we own the night.

Reverberations of Joy

In the laughter, echoes ring,
Every smile, a song to sing.
In the air, a sweet refrain,
Joyful rhythms, none in vain.

Sunny beams and brightened eyes,
In every cheer, the spirit flies.
Reverberate through heart and mind,
In our souls, true joy we find.

Moments shared, a tapestry,
Each thread woven meticulously.
In the fabric, joy entwined,
Echoes linger, love defined.

Through our laughter, hearts will soar,
In reverberations, we explore.
Harmony in every voice,
In pure joy, we all rejoice.

Symphony of the Soaring Soul

In the embrace of twilight's glow,
Dreams awaken, softly flow.
Whispers dance on gentle air,
Hope ignites, beyond compare.

Notes of laughter, echoes heard,
Guiding hearts with every word.
Harmony, a vibrant thread,
Connecting souls, where love is spread.

With every beat, the silence speaks,
In the stillness, strength it seeks.
Melodies drift, a sacred song,
In this place, we all belong.

Beneath the stars, we find our way,
A symphony that will not sway.
With open hearts, we rise and soar,
In this bliss, forevermore.

Veils of Sound and Silence

The hush of night enfolds the air,
Veils of sound linger, unaware.
Between the beats, a secret hum,
A silent drum that calls us near.

Whispers weave through shadows' play,
Echoes dance, then fade away.
In each pause, a story waits,
Glimmers of truth that resonates.

With every breath, the silence swells,
In depths of calm, a magic dwells.
Sonic waves in twilight's mist,
Draw us closer, we can't resist.

Sound and silence, a tender embrace,
In their dance, we find our place.
In twilight's veil, we lose control,
Finding our way to the heart and soul.

Spirited Currents

Beneath the surface, currents glide,
Whispering secrets, they confide.
With every pulse, the waters shift,
A spirited dance, a gentle gift.

Ripples echo, stories unfold,
Waves of strength, brave and bold.
In the depths, the silence sings,
To the rhythm of forgotten things.

Nature's heartbeat, raw and true,
Carves a path, leads me to you.
Each flow, a journey, wild and free,
Where dreams take flight, where souls can be.

Caught in currents, we lose control,
Though swept away, we find our goal.
In the waters' arms, we spark, ignite,
Into the depths, we dance through night.

Celestial Steps Across the Night

Under the moon's soft silver light,
We tread on dreams that take their flight.
Stars guide us, twinkling bright,
In the cradle of endless night.

Each step whispers the songs of old,
Tales of longing, daring and bold.
Through the cosmos, our spirits roam,
Finding in darkness, a sense of home.

A dance of shadows, light's embrace,
In this vast space, we find our place.
Celestial rhythms, sweet and wide,
With each heartbeat, we collide.

Across the night, the universe sings,
A symphony of endless things.
We are stardust, bound and free,
In this journey, just you and me.

Unspoken Languages of Silence

In the hush of night, whispers flow,
Words unspoken, hearts still aglow.
Eyes that widen, secrets unfold,
In silence strong, a story told.

Beneath the stars, thoughts intertwine,
A dance of souls, a silent sign.
Echoes linger in shadows deep,
The language of silence, a bond to keep.

Moments shared without a sound,
In quiet corners, warmth is found.
A gaze, a nod, a subtle touch,
In unspoken ways, we mean so much.

When words escape, hearts still can speak,
In whispered stillness, love feels unique.
Embrace the silence, let it thrive,
In unvoiced dreams, we come alive.

Tracing the Air

Among the leaves, the breeze will dance,
Whispers of nature, a fleeting chance.
Each breath we take, a story spun,
In the tender sigh, where dreams begun.

Wings of the birds trace paths so fine,
In the gentle current, we intertwine.
Every heartbeat, the air replies,
In the softest murmur, our spirit flies.

Clouds drift by, a canvas wide,
Chasing the moments that flow like tide.
In the silence between each breeze,
We find our hearts at perfect ease.

Tracing the air, we seek to find,
The echoes of laughter, the peace of mind.
With every breath, a memory made,
In the dance of the winds, our fears allayed.

The Grace of Memory

In the stillness of the mind, shadows play,
Fleeting moments, time's soft ballet.
Each note a story, a melody sweet,
In the heart's garden, memories meet.

Fragments of laughter, whispers of love,
Carried by winds from the heavens above.
In the dance of the past, we find our way,
The grace of memory guides each day.

Holding close the warmth of the days gone by,
In the folds of our hearts, their essence will lie.
Every heartbeat, a thread pulled tight,
In the loom of the past, woven with light.

As seasons change, we cherish the glow,
Of moments lived, the seeds we sow.
In the grace of memory, we learn to see,
The beauty of life, in each memory.

Rumors of the Past

Whispers of yesterday linger still,
In corners where shadows dance at will.
Echoes of laughter, tears long shed,
In the heart of silence, the stories spread.

Through the veil of time, a soft refrain,
Tales of joy, tales of pain.
Rumors arise from the depths of dreams,
In the echoes of history, nothing is as it seems.

Footsteps that falter, paths once bright,
Ghosts of the past still roam at night.
With every heartbeat, a whisper flows,
In the tales of the past, the present grows.

The winds carry secrets, softly they sigh,
Reflections of moments that flutter by.
In the canvas of time, we paint our past,
Rumors of the heart, forever to last.

Resonance in Twilight

In the hush of evening's glow,
Whispers weave through shadows low.
Stars awaken, soft and bright,
Spilling secrets of the night.

Breezes carry tales of old,
Silvery dreams in twilight fold.
Echoes linger, gently sway,
As daylight bids farewell to day.

Crickets sing a lullaby,
Underneath the velvet sky.
The world slows in still embrace,
Finding peace in twilight's grace.

As dusk lays its tender hand,
Nature breathes, a soft command.
In this moment, hearts unite,
Finding solace in the night.

Luminous Steps Unfold

With every step, the path aglow,
Footprints kissed by moonlit flow.
Set your dreams on starlit beams,
Let them dance in lucid dreams.

Whispers of the night surround,
In the silence, joy is found.
Gentle wonders lead the way,
Guiding hearts where spirits play.

Colors burst in vibrant hues,
With each heartbeat, feel the muse.
Luminous trails of hope and peace,
In their warmth, let worries cease.

Step by step, the journey calls,
In the light, our spirit thralls.
Together in this sacred night,
We find comfort, we find light.

The Pulse of Forgotten Melodies

In the attic, dust collects,
Hidden tunes that time forgets.
Softly hum a sweet refrain,
Echoes of a sweet, lost pain.

Strings of memory softly pluck,
Resonate with love's pure luck.
A melody, both light and dark,
In its rhythm, we embark.

Notes that linger, bittersweet,
Whispering where shadows meet.
Find the heart in every beat,
Let the echoes be complete.

Through the silence, stories rise,
With every note, the spirit flies.
In forgotten songs, we see,
The pulse of love, eternally.

Sway of Silhouettes

Dancing forms in evening's light,
Casting shadows, taking flight.
Figures drift on whispered breeze,
In the quiet, hearts find ease.

Silhouettes of dreams take shape,
In the dusk, our souls escape.
Glimmers of what could have been,
Woven in the night's soft sheen.

Fingers touch the air around,
In this realm, we are unbound.
Together in the dark we sway,
Lost in time, we fade away.

As the moon begins to climb,
Our shadows dance to whispered rhyme.
In this moment, we forget,
Life's sweet song, our silhouettes.

Ethereal Traces

In the misty dawn's embrace,
Whispers of the night depart.
Shadows dance in gentle grace,
Leaving marks upon the heart.

Clouds like dreams drift in the sky,
Painting tales of lost delight.
Stars above begin to sigh,
Ethereal traces in the night.

Softly glows the morning hue,
Awakening the world anew.
Nature's brush, a vibrant cue,
A canvas vast, a timeless view.

In the silence, echoes play,
Memories wrapped in beams of light.
Chasing shadows, lost in gray,
Ethereal traces take their flight.

Sounds of the Heart's Whisper

In quiet moments, whispers flow,
Echoing secrets from within.
A melody that few could know,
The heart's soft song begins to spin.

Rhythms dance upon the air,
Pulses resonate like sighs.
Every note beyond compare,
Bearing truths no mask denies.

Gentle strains of love's embrace,
Filling spaces, calming fears.
In this symphony of grace,
The heart's voice sings across the years.

With every heartbeat, songs arise,
Crafting stories, weaving dreams.
Listening close, no need for ties,
In silence, love's delicate streams.

Harmonizing with the Stars

Under night's celestial dome,
Stars begin their timeless dance.
Drawing souls from earth to roam,
In their light, we find our chance.

Each twinkle holds a secret spark,
Guiding wanderers on their way.
In the stillness, echoes hark,
Tales of old in bright array.

Aligning dreams with cosmic sighs,
We drift through endless realms unknown.
Every moment, magic flies,
In starlit paths, our hearts are shown.

Harmonies of night unfold,
Merging hearts with distant skies.
Whispers of the brave and bold,
In starlight, every spirit flies.

The Pulse of Forgotten Dreams

In shadows deep, the echoes fade,
Whispers of dreams once held so tight.
Fragments of hope in twilight laid,
Flicker softly in the night.

Memories pulse like a distant drum,
Calling forth what time forgot.
In the silence, we feel them come,
A gentle warmth in every spot.

Through the corridors of our mind,
Lost aspirations softly weep.
Yet in the heart, they still can find,
A rhythm deep, a promise keep.

Awakening the visions bold,
Reviving tales we long to weave.
In the pulse, our dreams unfold,
Whispering truths we still believe.

Choreography of Stars

In the quiet of the night,
Whispers of light take flight,
Each twinkle tells a tale,
A cosmic dance, we unveil.

Galaxies spin in grace,
Floating in endless space,
They beckon us to dream,
In their rhythmic beam.

Constellations weave their thread,
Guiding us as we tread,
With every pulse, we sway,
Lost in the Milky Way.

Stars hold secrets untold,
In their glow, we are bold,
For in the vast expanse,
We find our souls' romance.

Windswept Paths

Through valleys lush and green,
The winds carry whispers, unseen,
They weave tales beneath the sky,
Of travelers, dreams that fly.

Rustling leaves sing along,
With the breeze, they dance strong,
Every step on this route,
Echoes of joy, no doubt.

Clouds drift like thoughts untamed,
Each twist, a journey framed,
In the air, freedom sings,
As the heart takes to wings.

The horizon calls our name,
In the wild, we find our flame,
Together on this quest,
In windswept paths, we're blessed.

Reflections of a Hidden Dance

In the quiet moonlit glade,
Shadows flicker and fade,
With grace, they twist and turn,
In silence, we discern.

Beneath the stars, they play,
In a world tucked away,
A ballet of the night,
Veils of dreams taking flight.

Each movement, soft and slow,
A mirror's gentle glow,
Echoes of what we've missed,
In the tendrils of the mist.

As dawn peeks through the trees,
The dance remains a tease,
For in our hearts, it lingers,
A symphony with no singers.

The Echo's Gentle Caress

In the canyon, voices play,
An echo's soft ballet,
Whispers of the past reside,
In the shadows, they confide.

Mountains cradle every sound,
In their arms, we are found,
Melodies of time unwind,
In the depths of heart and mind.

Through the stillness, we hear,
Echoes drawing ever near,
In their touch, warmth we find,
Connecting soul and kind.

As the sun starts to rise,
Golden light fills the skies,
The echo bids goodbye,
With a soft, sweet sigh.

The Language of Celestial Bodies

Stars converse in silent light,
Whispers of the cosmos bright.
Planets spin in graceful dance,
Galaxies in timeless romance.

Nebulae paint the velvet sky,
Telling tales as they drift by.
Every comet writes a tale,
Of journeys through the cosmic veil.

In the dark, the moon will gleam,
Echoes of a distant dream.
Meteor showers, fleeting grace,
Illuminate the vast, dark space.

The universe, vast and grand,
Speaks a language we understand.
In wonder, we gaze above,
Bound by the stars, we feel their love.

Silken Trails of Sound

Softly the wind carries a tune,
Whispers beneath the silver moon.
Rustling leaves and distant chimes,
Nature sings in perfect rhymes.

Echoes dance in the twilight air,
A symphony without a care.
Birdsong mingles with the breeze,
Melodies weave through the trees.

Footsteps tread on path of dreams,
Every sound, a thread that seams.
Voices rise and gently fall,
In the silence, we hear them all.

In this realm of soft embrace,
Sound becomes a sacred space.
In the hush, our hearts align,
Connected through this sound divine.

Whirls of Nostalgia

Time spins back in gentle waves,
Memories drift in faded graves.
Laughter echoes, sweet and light,
Lost in a dream of soft twilight.

Familiar scents upon the breeze,
Bring to life forgotten trees.
Photographs with colors worn,
Whisper tales of love reborn.

Each moment holds a poignant trace,
Capturing joy in fleeting space.
We twirl in the whirls of yore,
Longing for what was before.

Yet in our hearts, their spirit stays,
Guiding us through winding days.
In nostalgia's warm embrace,
We find our roots, our sacred place.

The Melody of Embraced Echoes

In quiet moments, whispers play,
Lifting spirits, guiding stray.
Echoes dance on the edge of night,
Crafting dreams in silver light.

Voices blend in soft embrace,
Resonating in sacred space.
Every heartbeat, every sigh,
Weaves a tune that will not die.

Through shadows deep and valleys wide,
The melody remains our guide.
In the silence, stories bloom,
Painting colors through the gloom.

With every note, our souls entwine,
In the echoes, love will shine.
Together we find our way home,
In the melody, we are not alone.

Waves of Untold Stories

In the depths where silence dwells,
The ocean whispers secret spells.
Each wave a tale, a fleeting breath,
Of love and loss, of life and death.

Colors danced beneath the foam,
Carried dreams that found no home.
With every crest, a hope ascends,
A journey starts, as one begins.

The shores embrace the tales now shared,
Where hearts once heavy find they're spared.
As tides retreat, the truth will shine,
In whispers woven, yours and mine.

Listen close, the stories call,
In waves that rise, in waves that fall.
For in the depths and on the crest,
Lie wonders still, the heart's bequest.

Elysium of Echoes

In twilight's glow, the whispers play,
Dancing shadows, twilight's ballet.
Echoes travel through the glade,
Where memories of love won't fade.

Stars above like diamonds gleam,
A canvas painted, life a dream.
In every echo, stories blend,
Of lives once lived, of journeys penned.

The breeze enfolds a gentle sigh,
As fleeting moments drift and fly.
In every sound, a heartbeat's race,
A haunting touch, a remembered face.

Awakened hearts beneath the sky,
In Elysium's realm where spirits lie.
With echoes pure, our souls unite,
A symphony of day and night.

Melodies of the Mind's Eye

In shadows deep, the visions bloom,
A world created, free from gloom.
Melodies play in vibrant hues,
In endless dreams, the heart pursues.

Notes that shimmer, soft and bright,
Guide the soul through darkest night.
Each whisper sings of days long past,
In fleeting moments, love holds fast.

Through mind's corridors, melodies roam,
Crafting worlds where spirits comb.
In every tone, a story we find,
Unraveled threads that bind the mind.

Awake, asleep, let visions fly,
Into the realm of the mind's eye.
For in this space, we come alive,
In endless songs, our dreams survive.

The Rapture of Restless Feet

With restless feet, we roam and tread,
The paths unknown, where dreams are fed.
Each step a rhythm, pulse of the earth,
In wanderlust, we find our worth.

Through forests deep and mountains high,
Beneath the vast and open sky.
With every stride, a story forms,
In quiet hearts, adventure swarms.

From city streets to wild terrains,
In every footfall, freedom reigns.
The journey calls, the spirit stirs,
In restless feet, the heart concurs.

So take a step, embrace the call,
For in the rapture, we rise and fall.
In every wander, every beat,
Resides a dance for restless feet.

Rhythm of the Night Breeze

The moon whispers soft, a gentle sigh,
As shadows dance lightly, night draws nigh.
Stars twinkle above, like secrets they keep,
In the rhythm of night, the world falls asleep.

A breeze carries tales from far away,
Through leaves that shimmer, where spirits play.
Each rustle and hum, a lullaby sweet,
Guides the weary heart to rest and retreat.

The cool air embraces, a lover's touch,
While dreams weave their web, inviting us much.
In this deep silence, whispers arise,
Painting the darkness with luminous skies.

Caught in the magic, we lose track of time,
In the rhythm of night, our souls start to climb.
With every soft breeze, our worries unbind,
In this sweet moment, true peace we find.

Tides of Unwritten Verses

Waves crash ashore with secrets untold,
In the depths of the sea, stories unfold.
Each splash a reminder, of thoughts we neglect,
In the tides of unwritten, our dreams intersect.

The horizon beckons, where future shall bloom,
As currents entwine, dispelling the gloom.
Salt kisses the air, igniting the mind,
With every new wave, new meanings we find.

Across sandy shores, footprints erased,
Each moment a treasure, none to be chased.
With every tide turning, potential is cast,
In the ocean of chances, none should be passed.

Listen to the rhythm, the heart of the sea,
In the tides of unwritten, be wild and be free.
Let your spirit flow, like water it sways,
In this vastness of life, find your own ways.

Swaying Between Worlds

Between the realms where shadows reside,
A dance unfolds, with nowhere to hide.
With each breath we take, the fabric may tear,
Swaying between worlds, suspended in air.

The echoes of laughter, timeless as night,
Whisper through valleys, where darkness meets light.
In this delicate balance, our spirits collide,
Swaying between worlds, we learn to abide.

A tapestry woven with colors so rare,
Threads of our journeys, forever laid bare.
In the space in-between, we find our own grace,
Swaying gently onward, at our own pace.

With open hearts destined to wander and seek,
Through the layers of life, both tender and weak.
Embrace this journey, let intuition guide,
Swaying between worlds, where dreams coincide.

Vibrations of the Unseen

A hum in the air, a pulse we can't touch,
In the silence of being, it beckons us much.
With every heart beat, a rhythm divine,
In vibrations of unseen, our souls intertwine.

The flicker of light in an empty room,
Whispers of presence dispelling the gloom.
As shadows expand, we feel their embrace,
In the silence we share, we discover our place.

Intuition unfolds like petals in spring,
Each moment a note in the song that we sing.
With every connection, a story ignites,
In vibrations of unseen, we soar to new heights.

So listen intently, to the quiet call,
In the depths of the stillness, we find it all.
For in the unseen, our spirits are free,
Embracing the rhythm, just you and me.

Enchanted Footprints

On the forest floor, a path of light,
Each step whispers secrets, soft and bright.
Leaves rustle gently, a melodious hum,
Where dreams weave patterns, and shadows come.

In the twilight air, magic swirls near,
Footprints remain, drawn with hope and fear.
Echoes of laughter that dance in the breeze,
In this enchanted space, all doubts should freeze.

As moonbeams scatter, illuminating nights,
Every step forward ignites hidden sights.
Together we stride through this wild terrain,
Leaving our essence, like drops of rain.

When the dawn breaks and the shadows flee,
The footprints linger, a memory key.
Guardians of magic, they softly speak,
In every adventure, it's wonder we seek.

The Art of Floating Solitude

Drifting on water, a gentle release,
Where thoughts disperse, and whispers find peace.
A canvas of silence, the heart can explore,
In solitude's cradle, we long to soar.

The ripples create stories in rhythm and time,
Each moment a brushstroke, serene and sublime.
Beneath the blue sky, the vastness unfolds,
In this floating dream, the soul feels bold.

Soft breezes carry the weight of the day,
As we sail through the clouds, we drift far away.
With every soft wave, we learn to embrace,
The art of stillness, and find our own pace.

With stars as our guide, we wander the night,
In solitude's arms, we discover our light.
Reflective and free, we dance with the tides,
In the art of floating, our spirit abides.

Reflections on a Silver Lake

At dawn's gentle touch, the waters aglow,
Mirrored reflections in soft ebb and flow.
Whispers of nature, in harmony blend,
In silence we gather, where dreams never end.

Silver ripples echo, a song of the soul,
Gathering secrets that make us feel whole.
The sky paints a canvas, all colors unfold,
In the heart of the lake, stories are told.

Cedar trees lean in, their shadows embrace,
The laughter of breezes, a delicate grace.
Through tranquil moments, our hearts intertwine,
With reflections on water, pure and divine.

As twilight descends, the stars take their stage,
In this silver lake's glow, we turn a new page.
Each ripple a memory, each wave a song,
In reflections of beauty, together we belong.

Colliding Rhythms

In the pulse of the city, where dreams collide,
Beats of hearts echo, where shadows reside.
Each step, a heartbeat, alive with desire,
In the dance of momentum, we rise, we aspire.

Voices like thunder, a vibrant array,
In the swirl of the crowd, we lose and we play.
Threads of connection, woven through time,
Colliding rhythms, a beautiful rhyme.

Across busy streets, the stories entwined,
With laughter and sorrow, all hearts defined.
A symphony crafted from lives that embrace,
In the collide of existence, we find our own place.

As night draws its curtain, the colors ignite,
In the dance of the cosmos, we embrace the light.
Let's celebrate chaos, the pathways we roam,
In colliding rhythms, we find our true home.

Cacophony of Colors

Red screams in the morning light,
Blue sighs in the deep of night.
Yellow dances in the sun,
Green whispers when day is done.

Orange burns upon the sky,
Violet dreams that drift and fly.
Each shade sings a vibrant tune,
In the chaos of the moon.

Colors clash, a wild spree,
Blending 'neath the ancient tree.
A painter's heart, a canvas wide,
Where every hue can thus abide.

In this symphony of shades,
Life's complexity cascades.
Cacophony, a sweet refrain,
In the art of joy and pain.

The Dance of Whispers

Breezes carry soft secrets,
Through the twilight, gently met.
Leaves sway in a silent beat,
Nature hums beneath our feet.

Stars blink in a rhythmic grace,
While shadows softly interlace.
Echoes of the night unfold,
Stories of the brave and bold.

Each sigh wraps the world in lace,
Caressing time and hidden space.
Whispers weave a tapestry,
Of dreams that long to wander free.

In the quiet, hearts will dance,
Caught in fate's elusive chance.
With each murmur, souls align,
In the stillness, love will shine.

Timeless Variations

Moments stretch like slender strings,
As time to each heartbeat sings.
A clock ticks, its hands embrace,
Past and future, face to face.

Seasons change, yet remain true,
Each hue revealing something new.
Sunrise paints the dawn so bright,
While twilight folds the day to night.

Memories swirl in a dance,
Each glance a fleeting chance.
Eternal rhythms gently flow,
In every high, in every low.

Timelessness in every breath,
Life persists beyond its death.
In variations, we find peace,
Harmony's sweet, warm release.

Threads of Sound

Silken notes entwined in air,
Chasing dreams without a care.
Strings of voices play and weave,
Crafting tales we dare believe.

Rhythms pulse like heartbeats near,
Chords unfold, both bright and clear.
Echoes linger, softly bound,
In the fabric of lost sound.

Whispers swirl in gentle arcs,
Lighting up the darkened parks.
Melodies find their way in,
Echoing where love has been.

Each vibration, a tender thread,
Binding all that's left unsaid.
In every note, a truth profound,
In our hearts, the threads resound.

Unseen Partners in Flight

The sky whispers softly at dawn,
Wings brush the clouds, they're gone.
Silent calls, a dance in the air,
Unseen partners, lost in their flair.

Golden rays begin to gleam,
As shadows merge with the stream.
Together they glide, in graceful spins,
Chasing dreams where freedom begins.

Beneath the arch of blue and white,
They weave through currents, a stunning sight.
Nature's ballet, a story untold,
In the hush of morning, their secrets unfold.

In the flurry of wings, there's magic unseen,
Where boundaries dissolve, and souls convene.
With every flap, they defy the ground,
In the realm of the clouds, pure joy is found.

Rhythms of the Heart

In shadows of silence, beats arise,
Echoes of longing, whispered sighs.
Hands held tight, yet worlds apart,
We dance to the rhythms of the heart.

A gentle pulse, like waves on the shore,
Yearning for love, forever we score.
Each heartbeat a promise, soft and sweet,
Carried on breezes where lovers meet.

Through valleys of doubt, we stumble and glide,
Together in moments, where dreams collide.
The melody of souls, a vibrant spark,
Lighting the canvas, igniting the dark.

With whispers of courage, we take a chance,
In the silent glow of a tender romance.
Together we move, in time's gentle art,
Forever entwined, in rhythms of the heart.

Steps in the Starlight

Beyond the night, where shadows play,
We wander the paths of dreams away.
In the embrace of twilight's glow,
Every step leads where starlight flows.

With each gentle breath, the world feels right,
We dance through the echoes of soft moonlight.
Casting our wishes on constellations bright,
In the magic that blooms in the velvet night.

The whispers of cosmos call us near,
We listen closely, with hearts sincere.
Through celestial trails, we find our way,
Guided by dreams that refuse to sway.

With starlit steps, in harmony's grace,
We travel together, in endless space.
Each moment a treasure, as dreams take flight,
Forever enchanted, in steps in the starlight.

Reveries in Motion

In the quiet corners of the mind,
Reveries dance, they're unconfined.
Feelings like whispers, start to ignite,
Painting our souls in colors so bright.

Time drifts softly on wings of the breeze,
A tapestry woven with effortless ease.
Moments suspended, like leaves in the air,
Cascading softly, a vibrant affair.

With each fleeting thought, new worlds emerge,
Riding the waves of an inner surge.
Caught in the flow, we sway and we move,
Lost in the rhythms, our spirits improve.

In this vivid realm, dreams take their flight,
Boundless emotions, a wondrous sight.
Together we wander, forever in flow,
Finding our truth in reveries aglow.

Spirals of Sound

In the hush of twilight's grace,
Whispers weave through time and space.
Notes that dance on evening's breath,
Carrying secrets of life and death.

Shadows flicker in the glow,
Melodies echo, soft and low.
Each vibration a story told,
In spirals of sound, courage bold.

Harmony flows like a stream,
Braiding dreams within the theme.
Perceptions shift as echoes form,
Creating beauty in the norm.

As the night begins to fade,
Every note a serenade.
In the silence, still they cling,
Spirals of sound forever sing.

Chasing the Reverberation

Footsteps chase the fading light,
Through the echoes of the night.
Fragments of laughter linger here,
Chasing the reverberation, near.

Shadows dance on walls so bare,
Memories weave through the air.
Every sound holds a trace,
Of the moments we can't replace.

In the distance, voices blend,
Every note a twist and bend.
Through the silence, I will roam,
Chasing sounds that feel like home.

Time slips softly into dreams,
Chasing whispers, fading beams.
As the night unveils its song,
Reverberation, where we belong.

Echoed Steps of the Soul

In the cavern of the heart,
Echoes play their vital part.
Every step, a rhythm found,
In the echoed steps of the soul.

Paths entwined with hope and fear,
Carving memories so clear.
Footfalls softly mark the way,
Guiding light where shadows sway.

Voices linger in the breeze,
Carried forth through ancient trees.
Each resonance a gentle guide,
In the echoes, we confide.

Through the journey, strong we stand,
In the echoed steps, hand in hand.
Soulful whispers that we share,
Lead us onward, love laid bare.

The Ballet of Wind

Gentle sighs of evening's grace,
Whirl and twirl in a tender space.
Leaves pirouette on whisper's breath,
In the ballet of wind, no death.

Softly sings the nightingale,
Choreographed by the moonlight pale.
Every gust a dancer's leap,
In the arms of silence deep.

Rustling melodies caress the night,
As the stars gaze down with light.
Nature's symphony takes its flight,
In the ballet, pure delight.

As dawn breaks with a warm embrace,
Wind will lead us, time will trace.
In every whirl, we'll find our kin,
In the ballet of wind, we spin.

Moonlit Shadows' Embrace

In the hush of night so deep,
Whispers of secrets softly creep.
The moonlight bathes the world in grace,
While shadows dance in their own space.

Beneath the stars, a tender glow,
Hearts entwined, but few may know.
In this embrace, we find our peace,
As time around us starts to cease.

Echoed laughter on the breeze,
The cool air carries memories.
In moonlit dreams, we weave our fate,
Two souls combined, we navigate.

Together lost, yet found anew,
In every heartbeat, a love so true.
In shadows thick, our spirits rise,
Forever bound beneath the skies.

Threads of Unspoken Connection

Invisible strings pull us near,
In silence, our hearts hold cheer.
Unseen bonds in the quiet night,
Flickering sparks, a gentle light.

Every glance, a whispered word,
In a world where love's unheard.
With every breath, we share a sigh,
In the stillness, we reach for the sky.

Moments linger, soft and shy,
With unspoken truths that fly.
A tapestry woven, strong yet thin,
Through shadows deep, our souls begin.

Each heartbeat echoes, sweet and rare,
In the space between, we find our air.
Threads of fate, in silence spun,
In this connection, we are one.

Cascades of Celestial Movement

Stars cascade across the night,
Creating paths of silver light.
Galaxies swirl in gentle grace,
A cosmic dance through endless space.

Comets trail, bright and bold,
Tales of wonder, silently told.
In this vast expanse above,
We find the whispers of our love.

Nebulas burst in colors grand,
A swirling art, a painter's hand.
Each twinkle sings a timeless tune,
Under the watchful gaze of the moon.

In every pulse of the midnight sky,
A reminder that we can't deny.
We, like stardust, drift and flow,
In celestial movements, our spirits glow.

Lyrical Shadows in the Mist

In the morning's gentle light,
Shadows waltz, a fleeting sight.
Mist embraces every tree,
A silent song, just you and me.

Flowing softly, time stands still,
With every breath, we feel the thrill.
Nature's whispers, soft and shy,
In the fog, our dreams can fly.

Verses lost in the morning hue,
Echoes of a world so new.
In whispers, we find our way,
Through lyrical paths where shadows play.

Embracing life, each fleeting kiss,
In every moment, find your bliss.
The mist may fade, but love won't cease,
In lyrical shadows, we find peace.

Twilight's Embrace

The sun descends, a glowing sphere,
Painting skies with hues so clear.
Stars awaken, shyly they gleam,
In the arms of night, we dream.

The cool breeze whispers, soft and low,
As shadows stretch, and moonlight flows.
In this moment, hearts align,
Bathed in twilight's tender sign.

Crickets sing in rhythm found,
Nature's pulse, a soothing sound.
Every breath, a silent prayer,
In twilight's embrace, we lay bare.

Embraced by night, our worries cease,
In this stillness, we find peace.
Time stands still, in fading light,
Wrapped in dreams, we take flight.

Rhythm Beneath the Surface

In the depths, where secrets hide,
Waves of movement pull and bide.
A heartbeat thrums, deep in the blue,
Rhythms dance, unseen but true.

Bubbles rise like whispered dreams,
Flowing gently in silver streams.
Echoes carry, soft and slow,
The language only depths can know.

Currents weave a timeless song,
Inviting all to glide along.
In liquid arms, we lose our fears,
Beneath the surface, joy appears.

Together in this vast expanse,
We find our place, we learn to dance.
With every wave, a story told,
In rhythm deep, we feel the bold.

Whispers of Rhythm

In quiet corners, whispers sway,
Melodies of night and day.
A gentle pulse, a secret tune,
Unseen dances beneath the moon.

Leaves rustle softly in the breeze,
Nature's heartbeat, meant to please.
Each echo calls, a soft embrace,
In every sound, we find our place.

Footsteps merge on paths unknown,
In shared moments, we're not alone.
Voices blend, a harmony,
Whispers weave our tapestry.

Captured by this fleeting song,
We blend as one, where we belong.
In rhythm's arms, we lose all strife,
For whispers breathe the pulse of life.

Shadows in Motion

Beneath the trees, where shadows play,
Figures dance in soft dismay.
Flickering lights, a fleeting glance,
Life unfolds in shadowed dance.

The twilight weaves a silky thread,
Framing dreams of things unsaid.
In every flicker, a story spun,
Whispers echo, we become one.

Caught in motion, shadows weave,
Mysteries that we perceive.
Each twilight brings a new disguise,
As day gives way to starlit skies.

In this realm of dusk and dawn,
We find the magic that moves us on.
Shadows guide with tender grace,
In their embrace, we find our place.

Milton Keynes UK
Ingram Content Group UK Ltd.
UKHW022116251124
451529UK00012B/557